St. John Paul II

A Meditation on
Givenness

A MEDITATION ON GIVENNESS[1]

*"[I]n creating man as man and woman,
God imprints on humanity
the mystery of that communion which is
the essence of his interior life."*

---

[1] This meditation was originally signed on 8 February 1994 (six days after Pope St. John Paul II signed Letter to Families), but was not printed until 2006 (Acta Apostolicae Sedis 98, no. 8 [4 August 2006]: 628–38). Reprinted and translated with permission. The following footnotes are by the translator.

A Meditation On Givenness
Copyright © 2025 by Totus Tuus Press

Originally published in *Communio: International Catholic Review* 41, no. 4 (Winter 2014): 871–83. Reprinted with Permission.

All rights reserved. Except for quotations, no part of this book may be reproduced or transmitted in any form or by any means, electronic or mechanical, including photocopying, recording, uploading to the Internet, or by any information storage and retrieval system, without written permission from the publisher.

Published by Totus Tuus Press
PO Box 5065
Scottsdale, AZ 85261

Cover design by Devin Schadt
Interior design by Claudine Mansour Design

Printed in the United States of America
ISBN: 978-1-944578-12-1

FOREWORD

John Paul II had a deep love of nature and was fond to spend time in the wilderness, especially with young people. I vividly remember our walks in the Tatra Mountains in Poland and the Dolomites in Italy, where the beauty of creation naturally drew him into prayer. For the Holy Father, the goodness and givenness of creation was a reminder that everything is a gift from God.

In *A Meditation on Givenness*, John Paul II explores this same sense of wonder and gratitude, reflecting on what it means for one person to be a gift to another. He wrote this short but profound meditation in 1994, during the Year of the Family, and completed it less than a week after his apostolic letter *Gratissimam Sane*, addressed to families. Unlike *Gratissimam Sane*, which was widely distributed and translated, *Meditation on Givenness* remained unpublished until 2006, more than a year after the Holy Father's death. Although it appeared in the *Acta Apostolicae Sedis*, the official gazette of the Holy See, it remains largely unknown to the faithful.

In this meditation, John Paul II masterfully weaves together some of the central themes of his pontificate, including the theology of the body, human love, the meaning of gift, and the dignity of womanhood. I encourage you to pray over this remarkable booklet and to reflect slowly on the depth of its insights. I hope that this hidden treasure will soon receive the recognition and attention it truly deserves. May all who meditate upon it be inspired to discover the fullness of themselves through the selfless gift of themselves.

STANISLAW CARD. DZIWISZ
Cracow, February 14, 2025

1

CREATION AS GIFT

"Can one man[2] say to another, "God has given you to me"? As a young priest, I once heard my spiritual director say to me: "Perhaps God wills to give that person to you." These were words of encouragement, urging me to trust God and accept the gift one man becomes for another. I suspect it didn't immediately dawn on me that these words also hide a profound truth about God, man, and the world. The world, the very world in which we live, the human world . . . is the setting of an ongoing exchange of gifts—gifts

---

[2] In this meditation, the term *man* is used to translate both *człowiek* (*homo* in Latin) in some places, and in other places *mezczyzna* (*vir* in Latin). The two uses should be easily distinguishable depending on context.

given and received in many different ways. People live not only alongside one another, but also in manifold relationships. They live for each other; relating to one another, they are brothers and sisters, wives and husbands, friends, teachers, students.... It may seem that there is nothing extraordinary in this; it is just the normal pattern of human life. In certain places, this pattern intensifies, and it is there, at those points of "intensification," that this gift of one person for another becomes most real.

When two people join with one another, not only do they give themselves to each other, but God also gives them to one another. In this, God's creative plan is enacted. As we read in Genesis, God created the visible world for man, told him to subdue it (see Gn 1:28), and subjected the whole world of lower creatures to man's dominion. However, his dominion over the created world must take account of the good of individual creatures. The book of Genesis reminds us that God saw that all creation was good. Creation is a good for man so long as man is "good" for the creatures around him: the animals, the plants, as well as inanimate creation. If man is good to them, if he refrains from unnecessary damage or thoughtless exploitation, then this creation forms a natural environment for him. Creatures become his friends. They enable him not only to survive but also to find himself.

God, in creating, revealed his glory and gave the whole richness of the created world to man; he gave it to man for him to rejoice in it, to rest in it. For the poet Norwid—to rest, to restore, to reset, to renew—to *od-poczywać*[3]—denotes to be conceived anew, to be reconceived. God gave the world to man for him to find God in it and so also to find himself. Nowadays, we often speak of "ecology," i.e., concern for the natural environment. The foundational basis for such ecology, however, is the mystery of creation, which is a great and incessant stream of giving all the goods of the cosmos to man—both those goods he encounters directly as well as those he only discovers through research and experiments utilizing the various methods of science. Man knows more

---

[3] The Polish poet and author Cyprian Kamil Norwid (1821–83) noted that the Polish term for rest—*od-poczywać*—shares the same root as the words for "conceive"—*począć*, and "beginning"—*początek*.

and more about the riches of the cosmos, but at the same time he sometimes fails to recognize that these come from the hand of the Creator. However, there are times when all men, even nonbelievers, glimpse the truth of the givenness of creation and begin to pray, to acknowledge that all is a gift from God.

In the book of Genesis, we read that on the last day of Creation, God made man: "man and woman he created them" (1:26–28). "He created"—in this instance this means, even more profoundly, that God gave them to each other, mutually. He gave to man the womanhood of the woman who is of his kind, a "helpmate like unto him,"[4] and also gave man to the woman. So, since the very beginning, man has been given to the other by God. If we read the text of Genesis carefully, we find in it the very beginning, as it were, of this giving.

Man, as man, feels lonely among creatures that are not of his kind, and as such is confronted by a

---

4 Cf. Wednesday Audience Catecheses by John Paul II of 7 November 1979 and 14 November 1979 (John Paul II, *Man and Woman He Created Them: A Theology of the Body*, trans. and ed. Michael Waldstein [Boston: Pauline Books and Media, 2006]).

being who is like unto him. In the woman whom he receives from God, he finds a helpmate like himself (Gn 2:18). We must understand the term "helpmate" in its most basic meaning. Woman is given to man so that he can understand himself, and reciprocally man is given to woman for the same end. They are to mutually affirm each other's humanity, awed by its dual richness. On first beholding created woman, man must surely have thought: "God gave you to me." He said as much, though in different words—but he said as much (Gn 2:23). Awareness of gift and givenness is clearly written into the biblical Creation account. For man, woman is first an object of awe and wonder. With her appearance, the world first encounters what Gertrude von Le Fort termed "das ewig Weibliche": the eternal feminine.

2

GIFT AND ENTRUSTMENT[5]

"God has given you to me." As is apparent, these words I heard in my youth were not a mere random remark. God does indeed give people to us; he gives us brothers and sisters in our humanity, beginning with our parents. Then, as we grow up, he places more and more new people on our life's path. Every such person, in some way, is a

---

5 The Polish term *zawierzenie* can denote both entrustment in the sense of guardianship, placing the other into one's care, and in the sense of confiding in another or trusting in him or her. Over the course of this meditation, its meaning is explored at a series of levels. John Paul II writes of *zawierzenie* in relation to both Cain's question: "Am I my brother's keeper?" and the angel's words to Joseph: "Do not be afraid to take Mary to yourself." As the translator of this meditation into French, Pascal Ide has noted that in each of these uses, entrustment opens up to communion (see footnote 1).

gift for us, and we can say of each: "God has given you to me." This awareness becomes a source of enrichment for each of us. We would be in grave danger were we to be unable to recognize the richness in each human person. Our humanity would be in peril were we to shut ourselves up only in our own selves and reject the broad horizon that opens out to the eyes of our soul as the years go by.

Who is man? Genesis affirms at the very beginning that man is in the image and likeness of God. This means that a special fullness of being resides in man. As the Council teaches us, man is the only creature on earth whom God willed for itself (*Gaudium et spes*, 24). At the same time, he is the only creature that can fully find himself only through a sincere, disinterested gift of self (ibid.). Thus, there is a very deep connection between being for oneself and being for others. Only someone who has dominion over himself can become a sincere gift for others. This holds true to God's being in the ineffable mystery of his interior life. Man has also been called, from the beginning, to such a likeness in being. That is why God created him male and female. In creating woman, in bringing her to man, God opened man's heart to an awareness of gift, givenness. "She is from me and she is for me; through her I can become a gift because she herself is a gift for me."

I have often drawn attention to the fact that in woman is contained, as it were, the final word of God, our Creator.[6] For womanhood denotes the future of man. Womanhood denotes motherhood, and motherhood is the first form of entrustment of one man to another. The word "entrustment" is especially important here. "God wants to give another person to you" means that *God wants to entrust that other person to you.* And to entrust means that *God believes in you, trusts that you are capable of receiving the gift, that you are capable of embracing it with your heart, that you have the capacity to respond to it with a gift of yourself.* In this way, in creating man as man and woman, God imprints on humanity the mystery of that communion which is the essence of his interior life. Man is drawn up into the mystery of God by the fact that his freedom is subjected

---

6 Cf. *Mulieris dignitatem* and *Letter to Women.*

to the law of love, and love creates interpersonal communion.

God, man's Creator, is not only the omnipotent Lord of all that exists, but is also a God of communion. This communion is where that special likeness between man and God is played out. Through man, this likeness should radiate out to all of creation so that it becomes the "cosmos"—man's communion with all that is created and creation's communion with man. St. Francis of Assisi is one such figure in whom the truth about the communion of creatures found a special expression. The right and fitting place for communion, however, is first and foremost man—man and woman whom God has called from the beginning to be a sincere gift of self for one another.

3

APPRECIATION OF BEAUTY

Love has many facets. It seems that the first of these facets is a disinterested predilection, partiality, or liking: amor complacentiae. God, who is Love, bestows this form of love, above all other forms, upon man—a loving predilection. The eyes of the Creator, though embracing the whole created universe, rest especially on man, who is the object of his special liking. They rest on both man and woman as he created them. Perhaps that is why Genesis emphasizes that they were both naked and felt no shame (Gn 2:25).[7] Elsewhere,

---

[7] Cf. The detailed discussion of the phenomenon of shame in John Paul II's Wednesday Audience Catecheses of 12 December 1979, 2 January 1980, 14 May 1980, and 30 July 1980, and earlier in Karol Wojtyła's *Love and Responsibility* (Boston: Pauline Books and Media, 2013).

the author of the Letter to the Hebrews writes: "And before him no creature is hidden, but all are open and laid bare to the eyes of him with whom we have to do" (4:13).

God embraces man and woman in the whole truth of their humanity. He rests his creative and fatherly favor, predilection, in this truth. He grafts this disinterested liking, this predilection into their hearts. He makes them capable of mutual love, of a liking for one another. In man's eyes, the woman is a special synthesis of the beauty of all creation, and he too, similarly, in her eyes. Their nakedness is in no way a source of shame. It is deeply transformed by the love the Creator has for them. One can speak here of a certain special absorption of shame by love,[8] this time by the love of God himself. This love lets them interact with one another and rejoice in the gift of each other in all simplicity and innocence. It allows them to experience the givenness of their humanness, which always retains that dual modality of male and female.

---

8 This is one of the chapter subtitles in Wojtyła's *Love and Responsibility*.

It is worth noting that the words that institute marriage are not the first words the Creator speaks to man and woman. These first words speak rather of the bodily union of man and woman in marriage, as it were, from the vantage point of their future choice: man is to leave his father and mother and cling to his wife, become one flesh with her, and give beginning[9] to new life (Gn 2:24). From the very beginning, the preservation of humankind is connected with this order of God's creation. This very preservation, however, already presupposes a loving predilection. Within themselves, man and woman must first find a mutual predilection and discover the beauty of being human, and then their hearts beget the need to give new life—to transmit the gift of humanity to new beings whom God, in his own time, may give to them.

Anyone who judges that the biblical account of man's creation is dominated by biology is in great error. The Creator says: "Be fruitful and

---

9 *Dać początek* could also be translated as "engender," "beget," or "transmit," but the lesser-used phrase "give beginning" was chosen to better encapsulate both the giving, and the beginning in time, borne out by the Polish original.

multiply so you fill the earth and subdue it" (Gn 1:28), only after first having created within their hearts an interior space of loving predilection that is especially governed by beauty. One may say that in this way, in creating woman, God triggers that great aspiration for beauty which will become the subject of man's creativity, art, and much else.... There is a certain quest for beauty in every spiritual creativity, a certain quest for yet new forms of incarnation, new sources of wonder, which is as indispensible to man as food and drink. Norwid once wrote: "Beauty exists to awe us into work, and work exists to raise us from the dead." If man indeed rises again through work, through the different forms of work he carries out, this is precisely due to the inspiration he draws from beauty: from the beauty of the visible world, and within it especially from the beauty of womanhood.

This thread is woven into the whole history of man, especially the history of man's salvation. The culmination of this history is the Resurrection of Christ, and the Resurrection is the revelation of the greatest beauty, a revelation foreshadowed at the Transfiguration. The Apostles' eyes were awed by this beauty, and they wished to remain in its orbit. The beauty of the Transfiguration strengthened the Apostles so they could endure the humiliating Passion of the Transfigured Christ. For beauty is a source of strength for man. It is inspiration for work, a light that guides us through the darkness of human existence and allows us to overcome all evil, all suffering, with good, since hope in the Resurrection cannot be misplaced. All men know this—every man and woman knows this—for Christ is Risen!

The Resurrection of Christ initiates the renewal and rebirth of that beauty which man has lost through sin. St. Paul speaks of the new Adam (Rom 5:12–21). Elsewhere he speaks of creation's great thirst for the revelation of the sons of God (Rom 8:19). It is true that in humankind there is a great yearning and thirst for the beauty with which God has endowed man in creating man and woman. There is also a quest for the form of this beauty that finds expression in all human creativity. If creativity is a special way in which man expresses himself, it is also an expression of that yearning of which Paul speaks. There is suffering connected with this yearning, since "all of creation is groaning in the pangs of childbirth" (Gn 8:22).

The yearning of the human heart after this primordial beauty with which the Creator has endowed man is also a desire for the communion in which the sincere gift of self is manifested. This beauty and this communion are not goods that have been lost irretrievably—they are goods to be redeemed, retrieved; and in this sense every human person is given to every other—every woman is given to every man, and every man is given to every woman.

4

REDEMPTION OF THE BODY

These strivings of the human soul that are associated with longing for the beauty of the human person and the beauty of communion come up against a certain threshold. Man can stumble at this threshold. Instead of finding beauty, he loses it and begins to create only ersatz substitutes. Man can clutter up his civilization with these substitutes. It ceases to be a civilization of beauty because it is not born of that eternal love from which God brought man into being and made him beautiful, just as the communion of persons—of man and woman—has been created beautiful. Norwid, who had an immensely perceptive intuition of this truth, wrote that beauty is the form of love. Beauty cannot be created if one does not participate in that love. One cannot create beauty if one does not look with the eyes through which God embraces the world he created in the beginning and beholds man whom he created within that world.

All this is not to say that our era is devoid of people who strive for this with all their might.[10] We have never been short of such people. That is why the overall balance sheet of human civilization, so to speak, is after all still positive. This balance is created by the few who are great geniuses and saints. They are all witnesses to how mediocrity can be overcome, and especially how evil can be overcome with good, how good and beauty can still be discovered despite all the deprivation and degradation to which human civilization succumbs. As we see, this threshold over which man stumbles is not insurmountable. We need to be aware that it exists, and we need to have the courage to cross it ever anew.

How are we to cross this threshold? I would say that we must cross it by following our conviction that God gives man to man, and in giving

---

10 Cf. John Paul II, *Audience on the Occasion of the 180th Anniversary of the Birth of the Poet Cyprian Kamil Norwid* (1 July 2001).

man, he gives him the whole of creation, the whole world. When man discovers the disinterested gift that the other human person is to him, it is as if he discovers the whole world in that other person. It is important to recognize that it can happen that this gift ceases to be disinterested and sincere in the realm of the human heart. One man can become the object of use to another. This is the utmost threat to our civilization, especially to the civilization of a materially affluent world. A disinterested, loving predilection is then supplanted by the urge to take possession of the other and use him. Such an urge is a great threat not only to the other, but especially to the person who succumbs to it. Such a person destroys within himself the capacity to be a gift, and thus destroys the capacity to live by the precept: "be more a man"; he succumbs rather to the temptation of living to: "possess more and more"—more pleasures, more experiences, more sensations, fewer real values, less creative suffering for good, less readiness to sacrifice self for the good and beauty of humanity, less participation in Redemption . . .

It is by dint of our Redemption that the other

person—the woman for the man or the man for the woman—is such a great and inestimable gift. Redemption is rightly understood to be the settlement of the great debt that fell to mankind due to sin. Nevertheless, it is also, and perhaps mostly, a *re-giving* to man and to the whole of creation of that goodness and beauty which had first been given in the mystery of Creation. In Redemption, all becomes new (Rev 21:5). Man, as it were, is given his humanity anew in the Paschal Mystery, through Christ Crucified and Risen. Man receives anew his own maleness, femaleness, his capacity to be for the other, his capacity to be in mutual communion. This throws a new light on the words: "God gave you to me." God gives man to man in a new way through Christ, in whom the full value of the human person, that value which he had in the beginning, which he received in the mystery of Creation, is made manifest and present once more.

Each person carries within himself an inestimable value. He receives this worth from God, who himself became man and revealed the divine life that he confided, as it were, to man. Thus, he created a new order of interpersonal relationships. In this new order, man is even more so "the only creature on earth which God willed for itself" (*Gaudium et spes*, 24) and a personal being revealing a likeness to God, a being who can only fully find himself through a "sincere gift of self" (ibid.). Redemption, therefore, is the opening of human eyes to the whole order of the world that is founded upon sincere, disinterested gift. It is an order that is deeply personal, and also sacramental. Redemption affirms the sacredness of the whole of creation. It affirms the sacredness of man created as man and woman. The source of this sacredness is in the holiness of God himself who became man. As the sacrament of God present in the world, Christ transforms this world into a sacrament for God.

In the light of our Redemption, which was fulfilled through the sacrifice of the Body and Blood of Christ, the sacredness of the human body becomes more visible. This holds true even when that body is exhausted and trampled upon, just as Christ's was exhausted and beaten in his Passion. The human body has its own dignity, which flows from this sacredness. This is true of both the man's body and the woman's body. Redemption in the body gives, as it were, a special new dimension to the sacredness of the human body. It is a sacredness that excludes becoming merely an object of use. Everyone, especially every man, must be a guardian, a keeper, of this sacredness and dignity. "Am I my brother's keeper?" Cain asked (Gn 4:9), thus triggering the unhappy course of the civilization of death in human history. Christ comes into the midst of this civilization, into the midst of Cain's question and responds: "Yes, you are a guardian, you are the guardian of holiness, guardian of man's dignity in every woman and in every man. You are the keeper of the holiness of her body. It is to remain ever an object of your respect. Then you can rejoice in the beauty with which God has endowed her from the beginning, and she will rejoice in you. She will then feel safe under her brother's gaze and will rejoice in the gift that her womanhood was created to be." It is then that the "eternal feminine" (das ewig Weibliche) can once again be an inviolable gift to human civilization, an inspiration for creativity and a source of beauty given so that we can rise from the dead (Norwid). Is it not because of this that so many human resurrections find their source in the beauty of woman, the beauty of motherhood, that sisterly, spousal beauty which finds its special culmination in the Mother of God?

5

TOTUS TUUS

"Behold, you are beautiful, my love" (Song 1:15). If the Song of Songs is primarily a canticle about the love of human lovers, then in all its concreteness it is also open to many depths of meaning. The Church uses the Song of Songs in its liturgy, especially during commemorations of virgins and women who were martyrs for Christ. The cited words speak especially of the great radiance of the beauty of womanhood—not only, or at least not primarily, the sensual beauty of womanhood, but more so the spiritual beauty. One can also say that the latter is the condition for the former. Sensual beauty, by itself, does not usually survive the test of time.

As I have often experienced over the course of my own life, this is especially important for the person to whom God gives, entrusts another person. God has given me many people, both young and old, boys and girls, fathers and mothers, widows, the healthy and the sick. Always, when he *gave* them to me, he also *tasked* me with them, and now I see that I could easily write a separate book about each of them—and each biography would ultimately be on the disinterested gift man always is for the other. Among them were the uneducated, for instance factory workers; there were also students, university professors, doctors and lawyers, and finally priests and the consecrated religious. Of course, they included both men and women. A long road led me to discover the genius of woman, and Providence itself saw to it that the time eventually came when I really recognized it and was even, as it were, dazzled by it.

I think that every man, whatever his station in life or his life's vocation, must at some point hear those words which Joseph of Nazareth once heard: "Do not be afraid to take Mary to yourself" (Mt 1:20). "Do not be afraid to take" means *do everything to recognize that gift which she is for you.* Fear only one thing: that you try to appropriate that gift. That is what you should fear. As long as she remains a gift from God himself to you, you can safely rejoice in all that she is as that gift. What is more, you ought even to do everything you can to recognize that gift, to show her how unique a treasure she is. Every man is unique. Uniqueness is not a limitation, but a window into the depths. Perhaps God wills that it be you who is the one who tells her of her inestimable worth and special beauty. If that is the case, do not be afraid of your predilection. Loving predilection is, or at least can be, participation in that eternal predilection which God had in man whom he had created. If you have grounds to fear that your predilection might become a destructive force, don't fear it in a prejudicial way. The fruits themselves will show whether your predilection is for the good.

It suffices to look at all the women who appear with Christ, starting with Mary Magdalene and the Samaritan woman, then the sisters of Lazarus, and culminating with the Most Holy Virgin, who was blessed among all women (cf. Lk 1:42). You must never be prejudiced about the meaning of God's gift. Just pray in all humility that you may know how to be your sister's keeper, so that within the orbit of your manhood she might find her way to her vocation and sanctity. Once she is set free, she has the capacity for even greater courage and for openness to sacrifices that men often find it hard even to fathom. Acknowledging this, the Church repeats after the Song of Songs: "Behold how beautiful you are, my beloved."

Finally, it also needs to be said that this meditation on gift, givenness, has drawn on a long interior journey that has led me from the advice I heard from my spiritual director in my youth to the words *Totus Tuus*,[11] which have constantly accompanied me for many years now. I discovered these words during the war as I worked in the quarry in Solvay. I discovered them through reading the *Treatise on the True Devotion to the Blessed Virgin Mary* by St. Louis Grignon de Montfort. This was at a time when I had already decided to pursue my vocation to the priesthood, and so, while carrying out heavy physical labor, I also studied philosophy. I was aware that my vocation to the priesthood would put many

---

11 *Totus Tuus* means "All Yours: I am all yours, Mary."

people in my path, and that God would entrust each one of them in some special way to me: *giving* them to me and *tasking* me with them. It was then that the great need of Marian entrustment was born within me—that need which is encapsulated in the call: *Totus Tuus*. These words, first and foremost, are not so much a declaration as a plea that I do not succumb to any desire, however subtly camouflaged. They are a prayer that I remain pure, and thus transparent to God and to men. I pray that my vision, hearing, and intellect remain pure. *Totus Tuus*: they all should be at the service of revealing the beauty God has given to man.

I recall a quote from Norwid's poem, "Chopin's Piano":

I was with you in those penultimate days
of uncomprehended threads
Complete as a myth,
Pale as dawn,
When life's end whispered to its beginning:
I will not play recklessly with you, no!
I will only hold you up!

I will not play recklessly ... not tousle ... not ruin ... not belittle ... but raise up, praise, magnify ... *Totus Tuus*. All yours. Yes. We must ourselves be a total gift, a disinterested, sincere gift in order to recognize, in every man, the gift that he is, and to thank the Giver for the gift of the human person.

POPE ST. JOHN PAUL II II (1920–2005)
was canonized by Pope Francis in April 2014.

Translated by Maria MacKinnon

The original meditation can be found on the online platform Opoka: http://www.opoka.org.pl/biblioteka/W/WP/jan_pawel_ii/inne/medytacja_08021994.html.

I would like to thank Hannah Ashfield and Fiorella Nash for their close reading of my initial drafts and support in proof-reading. I would also like to gratefully acknowledge the work of Pascal Ide who translated the meditation into French—a language somewhat closer to English than the original Polish—in 2012. His translation was accompanied by a useful in-depth analysis of the text and its background (cf. Pascal Ide, "La 'Méditation sur le thème du don désintéressé' de Jean-Paul II. Une présentation," *Nouvelle Revue Théologique* 134 [2012]: 201–14.

TAKE A HIKE!

Before becoming pope, St. John Paul II
led hikes into the wilderness for young adults.
He brought portions of his manuscript
Love and Responsibility and explained
God's plan for human love.

We're doing the same.
Come on a wilderness backpacking retreat
and discover fellowship, faith, and
formation in God's cathedral of creation!

To learn more, go to JP2Trails.com

COMMUNIO
INTERNATIONAL CATHOLIC REVIEW

Issues on
Synodality
Crisis of Meaning
Poverty
Mediation
Health
Education
Happiness
Food
Nature
Tradition
Motherhood
The City
and more

Contributors
Hans Urs von Balthasar
Roch Kereszty
Robert Spaemann
José Granados
Angelo Scola
Jean Daniélou
Charles Péguy
Josef Pieper
Tracey Rowland
Jacques Servais
Rémi Brague
Madeleine Delbrêl
and others

Read, Subscribe,
and Find a Study Circle:
www.communio-icr.com

P.O. BOX 4557 | WASHINGTON, D.C. | 20017-0557
202.526.0251 | COMMUNIO@AOL.COM

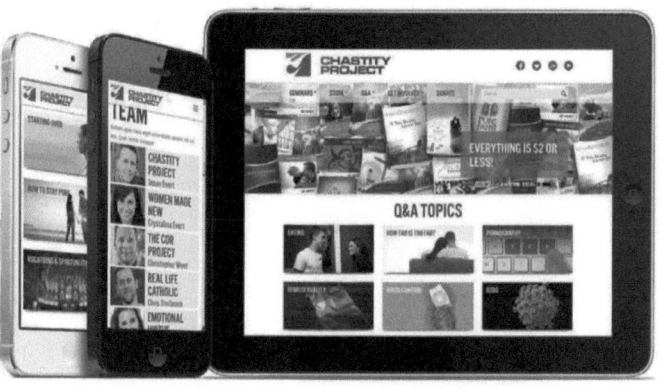

GOT QUESTIONS? GET ANSWERS.

WATCH VIDEOS
GET RELATIONSHIP ADVICE
LAUNCH A PROJECT
READ ANSWERS TO TOUGH QUESTIONS
FIND HELP TO HEAL FROM THE PAST
LISTEN TO POWERFUL TESTIMONIES
SHOP FOR GREAT RESOURCES
SCHEDULE A SPEAKER

Printed by Libri Plureos GmbH in Hamburg, Germany